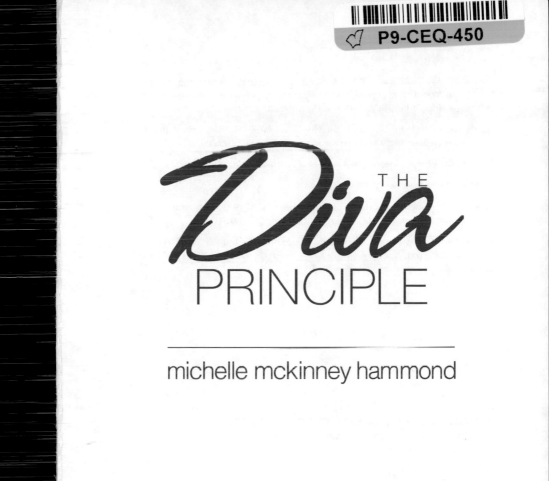

THE
Diva
PRINCIPLE

michelle mckinney hammond

HARVEST HOUSE PUBLISHERS

EUGENE, OREGON

Unless otherwise indicated, all Scripture quotations are taken from the *Holy Bible,* New Living Translation, copyright © 1996. Used by permission of Tyndale House Publishers, Inc., Wheaton, IL 60189 USA. All rights reserved.

Verses marked NKJV are taken from the New King James Version. Copyright ©1982 by Thomas Nelson, Inc. Used by permission. All rights reserved.

Cover by Koechel Peterson & Associates, Inc., Minneapolis, Minnesota

Cover photo by Tom Henry

Published in association with the literary agency of Alive Communications, Inc., 7680 Goddard Street, Ste #200, Colorado Springs, CO 80920.

Temperament assessments on pp. 52-54 appear courtesy of Dr. Tim LaHaye and his book *I Love You, But Why Are We So Different* (Harvest House). Used by permission.

THE DIVA PRINCIPLE—A SISTERGIRL'S GUIDE
Copyright © 2004 by Michelle McKinney Hammond
Published by Harvest House Publishers
Eugene, Oregon 97402
www.harvesthousepublishers.com

ISBN 0-7369-1389-0

Printed in the United States of America

04 05 06 07 08 09 10 / VP-CF / 10 9 8 7 6 5 4 3 2 1

Contents

Greetings, Divas!

ello, my dear sister. I am so glad you've decided to join me on this journey toward the fabulous, victorious life God has designed for us. Whether you decide to travel down this road alone or in a group study, I pray you will never be the same again. That as you begin to unfold butterfly wings and take flight, you will be able to celebrate your transformation and inspire others to join you.

It is important to keep in mind you will only reap the results you want by purposing to do the work that is necessary. Remember, faith without works is dead, dead, dead! Contrary to popular belief, transformations don't happen by osmosis—they usually come with struggle, determination, and persistence. We will jump though some emotional hoops, leap over some mental walls, and toss away some unhealthy habits.

I'm going to work you out, girl! I promise to make it as much fun as possible. Sometimes it might not be fun at all. Not to worry—consider it growing pains and move on because it's not about where you are right now, it's about where you're going and picturing the life you want to lead.

Getting into the victorious groove will take some introspection. Sometimes when we are taking an intimate look at ourselves, we are too close to deal with things objectively. That's where this guide will come in. Consider it your handbook for lifestyle design. It will help you separate fact from fiction, the majors from the minors. It will equip you to see the life that can be yours and help you reach your goals. By straightening out your thinking and using these practical guidelines and exercises, you will get on track and be on your way to experiencing victorious living through God's amazing grace.

Are you ready? I've designed this as a weekly study for either individuals or groups. These Life Design lessons are divided into three steps to help you internalize the principles on a deeper level. First, observation—simply seeing exactly what was said on the subject. Then, reflection—considering exactly how these facts are relevant to you. Finally, your "Div-otion"—how you will apply these learned principles to your life. Take your time, and if you need to revisit a specific chapter a few times to get it down, by all means do!

You will need your own personal copy of *The Diva Principle* (but of course!), a pen you love to write with (I just love those gel ones, don't you?), a journal or notebook (pick something pretty and befitting a diva!), and a Bible (I'll be using the New Living Translation throughout). Once you've got your materials, all you will need is a commitment to finish the course. A true diva finishes what she starts. How does she do it? By pacing herself. Therefore, decide right now to take this a step at a time—slow and steady wins the race.

May God bless you on your journey, girl!

Mind Design 101

*As a woman thinks
in her heart, so is she*
(Proverbs 23:7 NKJV, paraphrased).

✺ ◎ ✺

*A*ttitude is everything. The first thing we need to focus on is realigning our thoughts according to the blueprint the Master Designer has for our lives. As we gaze at this map, we will be able to visualize the finished picture and locate where the inward work needs to be done in order for the right foundation to be in place. Once that's in place, the stage for the outward makeover will be set. This is the natural progression of things...why it is so important to begin our Diva Lifestyle Design course by dealing with our minds. After all, a diva has got to have her head together, or she is merely a woman perpetrating "diva-hood."

*As a face is reflected in water, so the heart
reflects the person* (Proverbs 27:19).

Why are we talking about the heart if we're dealing with the mind? Because the heart influences the mind. It is the seat of our will. This is why God asks us to capture all of our roaming thoughts and emotions and bring our minds into obedience to Christ. The heart decides what it believes based on how it feels according to what it has seen or experienced or *not* experienced. However, we are not called to walk according to how we feel, we are called to walk by faith. This means we must adjust our thinking to line up with God's Word—our actions will then follow suit.

Let's see what God has in store especially for you—for your heart, mind, body, and spirit.

Solving the Mystery of Beauty

PREPARATION

Read *The Diva Principle,* pp. 13–26; and the entire book of Song of Songs. (Don't worry, it's a short one.) Focus on Song of Songs 1:5-6; 5:1; 6:4-10, and 7:1-5.

> *Mirror, mirror on the wall*
> *Who's the fairest of them all?*

Trust me, before Snow White's evil stepmother asked her mirror that question, she already knew the answer. If you have to ask, you already doubt yourself. This is usually the plight of most women. It is where the enemy likes to attack first. Why? It is difficult to celebrate others when you can't celebrate yourself. Now who do you think has the most accurate take on the issue of beauty? You got it! God. Let's take a deeper look at this.

OBSERVATION

1. What did the Shulammite woman think of herself?

2. Whom did she compare herself to? How did this change her opinion of herself?

3. What did the other women think of her?

4. What did the king think of her?

5. Who do you think was right about her appearance? Based on what evidence?

6. Whose report should she believe about herself? Why?

REFLECTION

If we read Song of Songs not only as the love story of a king and a Shulammite woman but also as an allegory of the love Christ has for the church, we can begin to apply its truth to our lives. I think it's safe to assume that after all the words of affirmation the king spoke to his beloved, she felt a lot better about herself. Unfortunately, if she never internalized what he said to her and took it to heart, the first person who came along to say something different or contrary to what he said would cause her to question herself all over again. We are quick to make assessments about ourselves based on how others react or respond to us. Why ask the mirror, which only reflects what we see?

When you look in the mirror, what do you see? Step closer, take a deeper look, and really study yourself. Wash off the makeup, get naked, and get real. This is important. See yourself as you really are. Skin deep and beneath the skin. Write down your first impressions—not your adjusted thoughts but your first reaction to yourself. Your first thoughts are truly how you see yourself.

List six things you don't like about yourself and why.

1.

2.

3.

4.

5.

6.

Now list seven things you *do* like about yourself. These can be inner qualities as well as physical features.

1.

2.

3.

4.

5.

6.

7.

Now list five things about yourself you would like to change. Why do you want to change each of these? How would these changes make you a better person? How would others benefit from the changes?

1.

2.

3.

4.

5.

Let's pull back a bit. What do others say about you? What is your reaction to what they say? Is their assessment of you true? Why or why not? Whose is the only assessment that matters?

Read Genesis 1 and Psalm 139.

What does God say about everything He created?

What six things does God know about you?

1.

2.

3.

4.

5.

6.

In what five ways is He actively involved in your life daily?

1.

2.

3.

4.

5.

How was God instrumental in your creation?

1.

2.

3.

4.

5.

DIV-OTION

Now that you know you are fearfully and wonderfully made, or purposefully created to be wonderfully complex, it's time to celebrate this awesome fact. Here's where your journal comes in. David wrote at the end of Psalm 139 these significant words: *"Search me, O God, and know my heart; test me and know my thoughts. Point out anything in me that offends you, and lead me along the path of ever-lasting life."*

I would like to add to that prayer: *"Show me anything in me that You take delight in as well."* As you pray this prayer I want you to...

- For 21 days, keep a journal of the things that God reveals to you on a daily basis about yourself.

- Write a prayer of gratitude for the unique things about yourself that come to light. Stick to one a day. It takes three weeks to form a habit, so at the end of this exercise, you should be feeling pretty good about yourself!

- Write the reactions of others to the change in you. People should notice the change because your attitude toward them will change.

- If a change doesn't occur, repeat this exercise again until it transforms you.

Diva Tips for Keeping Your Vineyard

Taking care of yourself is one of the greatest gifts you will ever give to yourself. In personal upkeep, it's the little things that count. Here are a few diva toilette secrets to keep you looking and feeling beautiful.

- Most soaps are harsh and drying. Find a moisturizing shower gel for showering.

- After showering but before drying, apply Johnson's Baby Oil Gel, and then pat dry for skin that will feel like silk all day long!

- To keep cologne or perfume soft and not over-powering, mix with an unscented body lotion or oil and then apply at your body's pulse points. The heat of your body will make the scent rise naturally without being too loud. This same trick can be used for the hair. Simply add a few drops or a spritz of fragrance to your hair conditioner, and smooth on.

- To keep your breath fresh, try internal breath mints. Most smells come from within depending on diet. Avoid coffee, onions, and garlic if you know you will be interacting closely with others.

- Hair looks better when it's clean and short than when it's long and damaged.

- If your nails are chipped more often than they're fully polished, opt for the *au naturel* look. File nails close and use a buffer to bring out their natural sheen. Clean and neat always looks good. The same applies to toenails. A neutral-colored frost seems to last longer on toenails if you must do polish.

- Make sure you are not allergic to your makeup. If you are experiencing mysterious breakouts, try hypoallergenic makeup, such as Neutrogena, Clin-ique, or Almay. Clean skin is a must in order to clear up acne and spotting. Make sure to remove makeup thoroughly at night. On days when you don't have to be "done up," use a good moisturizer and powder, instead of foundation, to give skin a rest.

- Keep your personal toilette simple so you can be consistent. You might have to change your skin products when the seasons change. Immunities can build up and cause your skin to react.

Solidifying Your Identity

PREPARATION

Read *The Diva Principle*, pp. 13–26; Song of Songs 2–4; Genesis 2:25; and Genesis 3:1-20.

As long as we are connected to the Lover of our Souls, our identity is complete and we live in a state of well-being with God, ourselves, and the world. But once we disconnect from the Source, we are plagued with self-doubt and feelings of insecurity. Our Father created us to crave connection with Him as well as with one another. The moment any of those pieces are missing, we find ourselves in search of affirmation and completion. The Shulammite woman experienced this same cycle but she's not the first. You got it! We've got to reach all the way back to the original Garden to get to the root of this issue. The answers lie with Adam and Eve, the epitome of innocence until....

OBSERVATION: SELF-CONSCIOUS

1. In Song of Songs, how does the lover describe his beloved, and what does his description imply about his comparison of her to other women?

2. Where did the beloved draw her strength from?

3. In what ways did the lover feed her?

4. Where did she draw her affirmation from?

5. What happened when the lover and the beloved were disconnected?

6. What did the beloved have to get past in order to find her lover?

7. In Genesis, how did Adam and Eve feel about themselves initially?

8. Who caused Adam and Eve to question themselves? How did he achieve this?

9. How did Adam and Eve feel about themselves after they digested the serpent's suggestion and offering?

10. What did Adam say about himself?

11. What was God's response to Adam's statement?

12. How did Adam's sin make him feel about his nakedness?

13. Because of the curse, whom would Eve look to for her identity?

14. Because of the curse, where would Adam find his identity?

15. Who named Eve?

REFLECTION

The serpent was able to convince Adam and Eve that God was holding out on them based on what they "lacked." Whenever we become self-conscious, we magnify our insufficiencies and begin to question God's love and provision for us. Perhaps God does not hand us everything we want or think we need because we would do ourselves more harm than good with it. Like a wise and loving parent, God only gives gifts that are good for us.

1. In what ways do you compare yourself to other women? Why?

2. Does your conclusion line up with how God sees you?

3. Where do you draw your affirmation from?

4. What do you need to get past in your own mind in order to make peace with how God created you?

5. In what ways are you self-conscious?

6. What things does the serpent cause you to question about yourself? About God?

7. In what ways do you sometimes feel naked? Is that God's truth for you? Is it your own truth or maybe even Satan's?

8. What does God offer if we can press past our own self-consciousness?

9. Do you find your identity in God or in a mate?

10. Do you find your identity in your work?

11. How much value do you place on being married or on getting attention from men as a way to affirm that you are a desirable woman? Why?

12. How much pressure do you put on yourself to perform well in the marketplace? Why?

13. What do you feel defines your self-worth and identifies you to others?

14. Where is the safest place to put our confidence?

15. How can we get over ourselves and refocus our confidence in Christ?

DIV-OTION

- In your journal, make a list of the things you really desire from God but have not received.

- Which one are you most deeply concerned about?

- What lies have you received about yourself based on this unfulfilled desire? About God?

- Decide if you believe that every good and perfect gift comes from God. Confess this: "No good thing will the LORD withhold from those who do what is right" (Psalm 84:11).

- Purpose in your heart to trust God with His divine timing and provision for your life. "Not now" doesn't mean "never" unless you desire something that would be harmful to you.

- Find a scripture that is appropriate to your situation. Write out a confession you will use whenever negative feelings or thoughts arise that cause you to question God's promises toward you.

Diva Resources

A Jewel in His Crown by Priscilla Evans Shirer

The Search for Significance by Robert McGee

Self Matters by Phillip C. McGraw

The Art of Facing the Masses

PREPARATION

Read *The Diva Principle* pp. 13–26; Song of Songs 4–6; and Judges 6–8.

In all honesty, we care deeply about what others think of us. The pressure is on in society to present a front of success and well-being to those around us. Whether it is by the show of material riches, fabulous clothes, the ultimate partner, or business success, a lot of who we think we are is drawn from what others think and say about us. However, we know that our outward display is not God's measuring stick of success. It is important to know that true success is measured by our relationship to God and the fruit that it bears. With this truth at work on the inside of us, the outside has to line up in a show of confidence and peace that others will be drawn to.

OBSERVATION: PEOPLE-CONSCIOUS

1. In Song of Songs, how does the lover affirm the beloved? What aspects of her physical beauty does he take note of?

2. What other attributes of hers have helped her steal his heart?

3. How do her love, words, perfume, and purity affect him?

4. What happens when the lover comes to visit the beloved late at night?

5. Why won't she get up to meet him?

6. What happens when the beloved does not readily respond to the call of the lover?

7. What happens when the beloved runs into the watchmen? What condition do they leave her in?

8. Where does the beloved go for help? Why does she need help?

9. In Judges 6:12, what does the Lord call Gideon?

10. What is Gideon's response? Why does he doubt that God is with him? Is this encounter real or imagined? Does it validate his doubt? Based on how the chapter began, what part did the Israelites play in their state of affairs?

11. What does Gideon say about himself? Where did he get this information from?

12. Where does God tell Gideon to place his confidence?

13. What does Gideon do to try to make sure he has God's favor?

14. What else does God ask Gideon to do before he goes into battle? Why was this important?

15. In Judges 7:1, why did God want Gideon to cut down the number of people in his army? How did God reveal who was unqualified to fight?

16. What assurance did God give that Gideon would win the battle?

17. What did Gideon and his warriors do against the enemy?

18. Who caused the warriors to fight and destroy one another?

19. What did the Lord's course of action give Gideon the confidence to do?

REFLECTION

In the story of the lover and the beloved, the lover's opinion of the beloved is based not just on her physical attributes, but on her inner qualities as well. Yet, something within the beloved makes her doubt that she can face him in any state. Only when they are separated does she take her eyes off herself and choose to focus on the beauty of the lover and recognize his value. In light of this, she forgets her own insufficiencies because something is now more important.

In the story of Gideon, the clay pots he and his soldiers broke remind us of our own frail humanity and insufficient strength. As the torches were hidden inside the pots, so the presence and unquenchable power of God resides in us. Israel used horns in worship as well as in warfare. When we lift up our praises and glorify God, acknowledging our weaknesses, He arrives on the scene in all His strength to defeat our enemies and set us free from the thoughts and circumstances that bind us.

1. What keeps us from resting in God's love for us?

2. In what ways do we try to make ourselves look good to God? To others?

3. What keeps us from being transparent with others?

4. Are you able to describe your relationship with God when others ask you about it? Can you justify your love for Him to others?

5. What did God call Gideon? What does God call you?

6. What seeds of doubt about God have you allowed to settle in your heart based on your past experiences?

7. Which experiences in particular have contributed to your frame of mind?

8. What lies have you received from others about yourself?

9. Is obedience crucial to feeling God's presence in your life? In what ways have you contributed to some of your past disappointments? Take your time with this one and be honest with yourself.

10. What beliefs do you need to get rid of in order to turn your thinking around? Why?

11. What does the fear of people do to us? How do other people's opinions keep us from moving forward?

12. How can placing our confidence in the wrong things or people hinder us from achieving the level of victory we want in our lives?

DIV-OTION

Knowing who you are is crucial to your existence. How far could you get transacting any type of business without your I.D.? You must also identify yourself whenever you begin a new relationship. Your identity is more than your name. What you know and how you feel about yourself will affect how you carry and introduce yourself. Your introduction will determine how others receive and respond to you. Now is the time to see yourself as you truly are and were created to be. Because this is such a crucial point, let's look at it from another angle to help you truly take it to heart.

- Take careful stock of who you are and write in your journal what you think of yourself. Make a second column telling how you came to this conclusion.

- Make a third list citing what others think or say of you. What are their opinions based on?

- Now, on a fresh page in your journal, select the good things from each of your columns and make them into a solid confession of who you are. Add what you would like to work on and ask God to help you develop in these other areas. Study and internalize what you've written.

- Make one final list of thoughts, people, and circumstances you need to be rid of or at least need to put into perspective in order to take your life to the next level. As you think about your life, lift and separate what is absolutely necessary from those things that are a distraction and hinder you from moving forward.

- Exercise wisdom in listing and carrying out your new priorities.

Diva Resources

God's Leading Ladies by T.D. Jakes

Seven Secrets Women Want to Know by P.B. Wilson

The Confident Woman by Anabel Gillham

Becoming a Woman of Beauty and Strength by Elizabeth George

WEEK FOUR:
Enhancing Your Reflection

PREPARATION

Read *The Diva Principle,* pp. 13–26; Song of Songs 6–8; 1 Samuel 15–16; Psalm 63; and Psalm 37.

> *But the LORD said to Samuel, "Don't judge by his appearance or his height, for I have rejected him. The LORD doesn't make decisions the way you do. People judge by the outward appearance, but the LORD looks at a person's thoughts and intentions"* (1 Samuel 16:7).

Most of us feel better about ourselves when we are sure we have something to offer to others. But the wrong offering or a gift offered at the wrong time can have very different results from what we expect. The right gift given at the right time is well-appreciated and precious to the receiver. The response we receive from the recipient can heighten our confidence and encourage us to give even more of ourselves.

OBSERVATION: GOD-CONSCIOUS

1. In Song of Songs, where did the beloved say the lover had gone? What was he looking for?

2. In spite of the beloved's lack of response, how did the lover feel about her?

3. When the focus of the beloved shifted, what happened?

4. What promise does the lover make to the beloved in his pledge of love and adoration to her?

5. What is the beloved's response?

6. What questions do the brothers ask of the beloved? How does she qualify her purity to her brothers?

7. What else does the beloved have to offer the king besides herself?

8. In 1 Samuel 15:10, why did God disqualify Saul from being king?

9. What was the root of Saul's problem?

10. How does people pleasing get us in trouble with God?

11. What is most important to God? (1 Samuel 15:22-23)

12. Take a look at 1 Samuel 16:7. What do people judge others by?

13. What does God look at when considering people?

14. In what way were all the sons of Jesse alike? What does the Scripture say set David apart from his brothers?

15. Consider David's writings in Psalms. Why might God have chosen to shower him with favor?

16. In what way was David a man after God's own heart? How did this qualify him for becoming king?

DIV-OTION

When the beloved finally realized what was important to the lover, she went in search of it. After she did so, she found herself surrounded by his presence and love again. She willingly offered herself to him without reserve. She could do so with confidence because she knew he would take delight in her purity. Her ability to offer him a fruitful place only added to her pleasure.

Unfortunately, not all of us live in the vineyard with the Shulammite woman. Our lives look a lot different. We've made mistakes, we've fallen, and some simply haven't mastered the art of finding out what is really important to God's heart. Like Saul, we can all justify why we do what we do, but if our actions are not pleasing to God, the consequences can be costly. Preserving self will always cause us to lose the very thing we cherish most. In our attempt to master life on our own and control its various scenarios, we feel as if we are losing more ground than we're gaining. This is when we must change our focus to yielding to the Lover of our souls—seeking to bear fruit and learning how to worship Him above all things. David had the heart of a shepherd and a heart for God. Because of this, he found incredible favor with God, who chose to promote him in the eyes of men.

> In your journal, make an honest assessment of your areas of weakness.

- Write down how these weaknesses play out in habits that are self-destructive.

- List the justifications you make to continue doing the same things.

- Try to find a scripture that addresses each of your habits and your justifications. Meditate on each scripture. Make it your daily confession.

- What does God say about what you are doing?

- In light of His Word, how solid is your rationale for the things you do? What results do your actions have on your life?

- Decide what steps you can take to change your actions.

- Ask a friend to hold you accountable.

- Focus on the benefits of doing things God's way. How will God's plan affect the outcome of your situation? Chronicle the positive changes.

Diva Resources

Sapphires and Other Precious Jewels by Terri McFaddin

Only a Woman by Terri McFaddin

Betrayal's Baby by P.B. Wilson

Longing for Daddy by Monique Robinson

Woman, Thou Art Loosed by T.D. Jakes

WEEK FIVE:
The Importance of Wisdom

PREPARATION

Read *The Diva Principle,* pp. 27–39; 1 Kings 3; 1 Kings 10:1-13; 2 Chronicles 9:1-12; and Proverbs 3–4; 8–9.

> *If you need wisdom—if you want to know what God wants you to do—ask him, and he will gladly tell you. He will not resent your asking* (James 1:5).

According to God's Word, wisdom is supreme. But wisdom is not just an accumulation of knowledge—it is understanding. We become wise not by memorizing information but by actually letting truth become reality in our lives. An experience or a revelation can cement what you've learned inside your soul. Therefore, wisdom is not merely intellectual. It is spiritual and experiential as well. A divine diva is the embodiment of wisdom. Small wonder God refers to wisdom in the feminine. Ah, but foolishness, or folly, is also characterized as a woman. Sometimes the difference between the two can be very subtle. Now let's take a closer look at the characteristics of wisdom and folly and how they can shape our lives.

OBSERVATION

1. In 1 Kings 3, what does Solomon ask God for?

2. What is God's response to Solomon's request?

3. What three things does God promise to give Solomon because of his request for wisdom?

4. What additional promise does God give Solomon for being obedient?

5. How does Solomon display his wisdom in judging his first difficult case?

6. What is Israel's response to Solomon's wisdom?

7. What prompted the queen of Sheba to visit Solomon?

8. What did she bring to Solomon?

9. What six impressions made the queen of Sheba conclude Solomon was a wise man?

10. What was her response to all she saw?

11. What three conclusions did the queen of Sheba make based on what she saw?

12. What four places does wisdom make herself accessible to all? (Proverbs 8:2-3)

13. What two gifts does wisdom want to give to us? (Proverbs 8:5)

14. What are the six characteristics of the things she has to say? (Proverbs 8:6-9)

15. What seven things does wisdom have ready access to (Proverbs 8:12-14)? Perhaps these are the seven pillars of her house (Proverbs 9:1). Look up the definition of each one.

16. What four rewards are the results of heeding wisdom's advice? (Proverbs 8:15-16)

17. What four things does wisdom have to distribute to others?

18. What six things do you receive when you love and seek wisdom?

19. What was already in existence before God created anything else? (Proverbs 8:22-23)

20. What are the four characteristics of folly? (Proverbs 9:13)

21. Who does folly invite to her house? (Proverbs 9:14-16)

22. What does folly have to offer? (Proverbs 9:17)

23. What are the effects of her dinner on those who attend?

24. What are the two things that wisdom and folly both do?

25. Contrast their motivation for inviting people to their house?

REFLECTION

If it is true that a wise woman builds her house, but a foolish woman tears hers down with her own hands (Proverbs 14:1), then truly gaining wisdom and understanding should be at the top of our list of priorities. Without wisdom, we are not equipped to build the foundation of faith or life we want. The book of Proverbs is an excellent heads-up on basic wisdom for everyday living and for making our spirituality a practical reality.

Read Proverbs 3–4.

1. Which scripture spoke the loudest to you?

2. What is the instruction you need to follow?

3. What is the wisdom of this instruction?

4. What understanding do you get out of this verse?

5. What good judgment comes out of this?

6. What discernment will you need?

7. What knowledge have you gained?

8. What discretion will you now exercise?

9. What is God saying directly to you through this specific lesson?

DIV-OTION

List the Do's and Don'ts in Proverbs 3 and 4.

DO   DON'T

- Which Do's and Don'ts apply directly to you?

- In your journal, write a faith confession for renewal in this area in your own life.

Diva Resources

God's Wisdom for a Woman's Life by Elizabeth George

Being a Wise Woman in a Wild World by Robin Chaddock

The 10 Best Decisions a Woman Can Make by Pam Farrel

Recognizing the Value of Others

PREPARATION

Read *The Diva Principle*, pp. 41–52; and Judges 1–5.

> *As God's messenger, I give each of you this warning. Be honest in your estimate of yourselves, measuring your value by how much faith God has given you. Just as our bodies have many parts and each part has a special function, so it is with Christ's body. We are all parts of his one body, and each of us has different work to do. And since we are all one body in Christ, we belong to each other, and each of us needs all the others* (Romans 12:3-5).

If we are not secure in who we are and knowledgeable about our gifts, it will be difficult to share successes with others and even more difficult to empower others to excel in their own right. One of the greatest tools of empowerment we possess is the gift of encouragement. Women have the unique insight of being able to locate the strengths of others and activate them. Sometimes our own insecurities cause us to withhold encouraging words from others that would not only make them better men, women, and children, but also make us greater vessels of blessing as well.

The bottom line is that we need one another in order to live a victorious life. We all have different strengths and weaknesses, but we need to balance them between us. As we learn to celebrate the strengths of others and encourage them to bring their gifts to light, we will find ourselves empowered. We can then share more victories between us, more than if we fought alone. Later on, we'll be researching how our personalities factor into the equation.

OBSERVATION

1. What were the three callings on Deborah's life? (Judges 4:5) Pay attention to the order listed.

    a.

    b.

    c.

2. What were the orders that she gave to Barak? On whose authority did she speak?

3. Why would Barak want Deborah to go with him to the battlefield?

4. What did his unwillingness to trust God and go alone cost him?

5. How did Deborah give Barak the lead in the fight against Sisera?

6. Jael killed the enemy, but what did Deborah do to acknowledge Barak's part in the battle?

REFLECTION

> *Two people can accomplish more than twice as much as one; they get a better return for their labor. If one person falls, the other can reach out and help. But people who are alone when they fall are in real trouble. And on a cold night, two under the same blanket can gain warmth from each other. But how can one be warm alone? A person standing alone can be attacked and defeated, but two can stand back-to-back and conquer. Three are even better, for a triple-braided cord is not easily broken* (Ecclesiastes 4:9-12).

No man or woman is an island. God created us to be dependent—first on Him, then on others. Because we each have different gifts and strengths, we must learn how to balance all of our assets between us. To be able to recognize not only what we have to offer to others, but what others bring to the table in our lives, is the secret to gaining priceless victories you could never master alone.

1. What keeps us from seeking help from others?

2. What does the Word of God say about pride?

3. How does fear hinder our faith?

4. How does a lack of faith stop us from gaining God's promises?

5. How was Deborah a help to Barak? How could she have been a hindrance?

6. What was the greatest thing she did to enable Barak in battle?

7. Why is it important to force people to rise to the occasion? Is rescuing them always helpful?

8. How can you know when to assist and when to step back?

MORE REFLECTION

Our personalities define how we deal with other people. When taking a look at yourself, you need to look within at your temperament. Have you ever asked yourself, "Why am I the way I am?" "Why do I react/respond to things in the manner I do?" "Why can't I be more this way or that?" Well, it all has to do with the way you were designed—your temperament. Most people have a particular kind of temperament. You can also be a blend of different temperaments, with one being more dominant. A study on temperaments can help unlock valuable keys to your inner identity and give you a greater understanding of who you are.

In order to use our personalities to glorify God and bless the people around us, we've got to be completely honest with ourselves. This calls for a long look at the inner mirror of our hearts to see exactly what resides there. The Holy Spirit is always willing to assist and shed light on the areas we've tucked away or overlooked. For those who are brave enough to do the internal work, the rewards are endless. Knowing the truth gives us the ability to free ourselves from mind-sets, emotions, and habits that bind us and keep us from experiencing the type of life we really want to live. Let's dig deep and get real—with God and ourselves.

Make a list of your weaknesses.

1.

2.

3.

4.

5.

Now make a list of your strengths.

1.

2.

3.

4.

5.

Make a list of habits you think keep you from moving forward or mind-sets that keep you stuck in the past.

1.

2.

3.

4.

5.

What emotions would you like to have greater control of?

Now let's explore what Dr. Tim LaHaye has researched on temperaments and how it can help you gain greater insight about yourself.

Understanding what makes you tick is vital to harnessing your inner strengths and directing your life choices. By knowing where your areas of weakness are, you can work to improve them and avoid situations that would exploit them. Dr. LaHaye lists the four main temperaments in his book, *I Love You, But Why Are We So Different?*

Below is a list of these four types with their strengths and weaknesses.

Sanguine

Sanguines are by far the most extroverted. They are fun-loving and emotionally charged. They often suffer from a lack of discipline.

Strengths	Weaknesses
People-person	Lacking in discipline
Enthusiastic	Emotionally excitable
Talkative	Unstable
Compassionate	Disorganized
Ambitious	Restless

Choleric

Cholerics are natural-born leaders. They are decisive and focused. They can be extremely motivational and are great at long-term planning. Cholerics tend to be quick-tempered and stubborn when things don't go their way.

Strengths	Weaknesses
Independent	Impatient
Practical	Sarcastic
Active	Domineering
Confident	Opinionated
Productive	Volatile

Melancholy

Melancholies are more introverted. They tend to be lovers of the arts and very creative. They are analytical and highly organized. Melancholies tend to be self-critical and pessimistic.

Strengths	Weaknesses
Self-sacrificing	Moody
Industrious	Critical
Sensitive	Impractical

Strengths	Weaknesses
Loyal	Deeply emotional
Perfectionist	Suspicious

Phlegmatic

Phlegmatics are soft-spoken, gentle people. They are very supportive and incredibly dependable. Phlegmatics tend to sidestep confrontation and can be difficult to motivate.

Strengths	Weaknesses
Calm	Passive
Objective	Indecisive
Agreeable	Unsure
Humorous	Lazy
Dependable	Selfish

Did you identify with some of these? Discovering what your temperament is will allow you to see how you interact with other people. Do you quickly lose your patience with someone who is indecisive? Are you a day-dreamer who finds it hard to focus on the task at hand? This is important stuff, girl. Make sure you dedicate some study time to learning more about yourself so you can have an even more victorious attitude.

It's also beneficial to know what your spiritual gifts are. Take the following test to locate your strengths and specific spiritual gifts, and identify the gifts and strengths of others.

God has given everyone certain gifts. Some people are born leaders or teachers. Others work behind the scenes, uplifting others with their acts of service and unselfish giving. Knowing your gifts can give you a better perspective on all aspects of your life—from your career choice to how you relate to your family.

The abbreviated questionnaire below is a condensed version of the Motivational Gift Adult Questionnaire, but it should give you some idea of where your strengths and weaknesses may lie. I strongly encourage you to explore your gifting more thoroughly after this initial introduction. Take a look at *Discover Your God-Given Gifts,* by Don and Katie Fortune (Baker Books) from which this partial assessment is taken and used here by permission. This abbreviated form of the questionnaire is copyrighted and may not be copied or duplicated in any form.

On a scale of 0 (never) to 10 (always), rate the characteristics listed below each gift. Add up the total at the bottom of each section.

Teaching   Score

Validates truth by checking out all the facts.   _____

Loves to study and do research.   _____

Is more objective than subjective.   _____

Emphasizes facts and the accuracy of words.   _____

Solves problems by starting with
    scriptural principles.   _____

Is self-disciplined.   _____

Has only a select circle of friends.   _____

Believes truth has the intrinsic power
    to produce change.   _____

Is slow to accept viewpoints of others.   _____

Tends to be legalistic.   _____

                                        Total: _____

Administration   Score

Is highly motivated to organize that for which
    she's responsible.   _____

Expresses ideas in ways that communicate
    clearly.   _____

Prefers to be under authority in order
  to have authority.   _____

Enjoys working on long-range goals
  and projects.   _____

Is a natural and capable leader.   _____

Likes working with and being around people.   _____

Is a visionary person with a broad perspective.   _____

Has great zeal and enthusiasm for whatever
  she is involved in.   _____

Becomes upset when others don't share
  her vision.   _____

Tends to be driven and can neglect relationships.   _____

                                           Total: _____

Giving   Score

Gives freely of money, possessions, time,
  energy, and love.   _____

Loves to give without others knowing it.   _____

Gives to support and bless others or to
  advance a ministry.   _____

Views hospitality as an opportunity to give.   _____

Handles finances with wisdom and frugality.   _____

Is very industrious with a tendency toward
  success.   _____

Has natural and effective business ability.   _____

Likes to get the best value for the money
  spent.   _____

May try to control how contributions are used.   _____

May use financial giving to get out of other
  responsibilities.   _____

                                           Total: _____

Exhortation   Score

Loves to encourage others to live victoriously.   _____

Prefers to apply truth rather than research it.   _____

Focuses on working with people.   _____

Loves to do personal counseling.   _____

Is fluent in communication.   _____

Views trials as opportunities to produce
    personal growth.   _____

Makes decisions easily.   _____

Always completes what is started.   _____

Tends to interrupt others in eagerness to give
    opinion or advice.   _____

Can be overly self-confident.   _____

                                                                 Total: _____

Serving   Score

Easily recognizes practical needs and is quick
    to meet them.   _____

Is a detail person with a good memory.   _____

Enjoys showing hospitality.   _____

Has a hard time saying no to requests for help.   _____

Shows love for others in deeds and actions
    more than words.   _____

Does not want to lead others or projects.   _____

Has a high energy level.   _____

Supports others who are in leadership.   _____

Tends to be a perfectionist.   _____

Is easily hurt when unappreciated.   _____

                                                                 Total: _____

Perception   Score

Quickly and accurately identifies good and
evil and hates evil.   _____

Sees everything as either black or white. No
gray areas.   _____

Has only a few or no close friends.   _____

Views the Bible as the basis for truth, belief,
action, and authority.   _____

Is frank and outspoken, and doesn't mince
words.   _____

Is a very persuasive speaker.   _____

Has strong opinions and convictions.   _____

Has strict personal standards.   _____

Tends to be judgmental and blunt.   _____

Struggles with self-image problems.   _____

Total: _____

Compassion   Score

Has tremendous capacity to show love.   _____

Always looks for good in people.   _____

Is attracted to people who are hurting or
in distress.   _____

Takes care with words and actions to avoid
hurting others.   _____

Easily detects insincerity or wrong motives.   _____

Is trusting and trustworthy.   _____

Avoids conflicts and confrontations.   _____

Is ruled by the heart rather than head.   _____

Is easily hurt by others.   _____

Affectionate nature is often misinterpreted by
opposite sex.   _____

Total: _____

In the box below, shade in your totals from each of the gifts. This will allow you to see what areas you excel in and what areas you're not as comfortable in. *6 – 2 – 06*

	10	20	30	40	50	60	70	80	90	100
Perceiver							▓			
Server			▓							
Teacher							▓			
Exhorter						▓				
Giver	▓									
Administrator					▓					
Compassion						▓				

You can order the books and questionnaires directly from the authors by calling toll-free (866) 395-2291. For more details and a complete listing of materials, visit their website: www.heart2heart.org or email them: fortune@heart2heart.org

DIV-OTION

- ~ In your journal, make a list of your favorite strengths and how they can benefit yourself and others. Identify a potential weakness that could dilute your strength and its effect on others.

- ~ Make a list of your gifts.

- ~ Now explore the jobs or ministries you can apply these gifts to. Which ones on your list spark your interest? Are you actively doing any of them right now? Why not?

- Assess how happy you are with your present vocation. Are you using your gifts in the job you have right now?

- Make a list of ways you can incorporate more of your gifts in your job.

- Have you always wanted to start a business for yourself? Write down what has kept you from doing it. Now make a list of things you can begin to do to make your dream come true.

- Write down a plan for utilizing your gifts to bless others and prosper yourself. Make a mental note to revisit this list every few months and journal your progress.

Diva Resources

Jesus CEO by Laurie Beth Jones

The Power of Influence by John Maxwell

Listen to Your Life by Valerie Burton

I Love You, But Why Are We So Different by Tim LaHaye

Why You Act the Way You Do by Tim LaHaye

The Birth Order Book by Kevin Leman

The Spirit-Controlled Woman by Beverly LaHaye

Discover Your God-Given Gifts by Don and Katie Fortune

Discover Your Spouse's Gifts by Don and Katie Fortune

Heart Design 101

My child, listen and be wise. Keep
your heart on the right course
(Proverbs 23:19).

% ⊚ ℘

*I*f it's true that "out of the abundance of the heart the mouth speaks," then truly our actions arise from the seat of this very powerful throne. Let's face it—our heart has the ability to rule us. For those who are truly passionate, our hearts can be our undoing. It is crucial that we master its longings and its responses. How we feel cements our thoughts, forms our words, and shapes our actions.

How does a diva keep her heart in the right place? By seeking out the wisdom of God and allowing herself to be cleansed by His Word. By adjusting her attitude and paving the way for the life she longs for and dreams about. It's up to us to master our heart.

Just as we are told to choose life or death, blessings or curses, we get to chooses our heart condition. A wise diva chooses joy, chooses to trust God. Choose to walk in peace, knowing that you may not be certain what tomorrow holds, but you definitely know Who holds tomorrow. Choose faith over fear, fruitfulness over barrenness of spirit, balance over being overextended. Your heart condition has everything to do with the quality of your health and your ability to handle life. Take the necessary steps to nurture it.

> *A cheerful heart is good medicine, but a broken spirit saps a person's strength* (Proverbs 17:22).

Cultivating the Girl of Fruitfulness

PREPARATION

Read *The Diva Principle,* pp. 55–67; Book of Ruth; Genesis 29:31–30:24; and Jeremiah 29:4-14.

The reality of everyday living is that life happens. Many times our best-laid plans are thwarted by unforeseen circumstances and interruptions. These situations can wreak havoc on our emotions, causing us to behave impulsively and endanger our mental, spiritual, and physical health. When we do, we lower our capacity to be productive and victorious in spite of unpleasant or undesirable occurrences. Loss happens, disappointment happens. Sometimes we feel we are in bondage to our situations, yet we must rise above our trials and continue onward. In the cycle of life, we are forced to begin again and again. How we proceed is up to us.

OBSERVATION

1. What was the turning point in Ruth's life?

2. What attitude could Ruth have taken toward her loss?

3. What attitude did Ruth take?

4. What separated Ruth from her sister-in-law, Orpah? What was Orpah's motivation for going to Judah? What changed her mind about going? What was Ruth's motivation for going to Judah?

5. What steps did Ruth take to survive in spite of her lack or grief?

6. What was Ruth's reward for her perseverance?

7. Why do you believe God rewarded her in such a way?

8. In Genesis 29:31–30:2, what eluded Leah?

9. How did Leah think she could gain her husband's love? Was she right?

10. What was Leah's conclusion once she realized that having children did not change his heart toward her?

11. Why do you think Leah stopped having children after she decided to focus on praising the Lord?

12. Who did Rachel blame for her inability to have children? Was that an accurate conclusion?

13. Who did Jacob blame for Rachel's barrenness? Was his statement valid? Why?

In Jeremiah 29, the Israelites found themselves in a difficult situation. They felt trapped and helpless. They hoped that God would magically make a way for them to get out of their situation, yet He did not. Instead, He gave them a plan for dealing with their situation.

1. What were the first four things they were to do?

2. Why was it important for the Israelites to plan to stay?

3. Why was it important to grow food and stay healthy?

4. Why was it important for the Israelites to pay attention to their personal well-being in this situation?

5. What four relational things were they instructed to do?

6. Why was it important for the Israelites to work on their relationships in this difficult place?

7. What four societal things were they encouraged to pay attention to?

8. Why was it important for the Israelites to contribute to the society they found themselves in?

9. What two things were they instructed not to do?

10. What was the reality of their situation?

11. What did God promise the Israelites would happen after they had completed their season of captivity?

12. What were God's plans for them?

13. What were the Israelites instructed to do in order to get God's attention?

14. What four things did He promise to do for them once they changed their priorities?

REFLECTION

No one escapes the pain of loss. Unexpected circumstances can interrupt our lives at any time and cause us to question our future joy and security. We can't just sit on the sidelines of life when this occurs. After a grieving period, we must make important decisions. Just as the team who has lost a game is expected to play again, we must move on. Adjusting our attitude and solidifying our outlook are crucial. We must never run from the One who can help us most, nor should we feel that we must shoulder the burden of beginning again alone.

1. What needs in our lives does the Lord fulfill when we shift our focus back to Him?

2. Are you tempted to blame someone else for situations in your life—someone who can do nothing about them?

3. Who is ultimately in control of your circumstances? How does this change your perspective on your trial?

4. How can refusing to accept the reality of your situation keep you from moving forward and gaining victory?

5. What does the truth equip us with in difficult situations?

6. What is your attitude toward God in times of crisis and disappointment?

7. What does God's Word say His intentions are toward us? Do you believe this?

8. What stops you from having a complete assurance of His love and His good intentions toward you?

9. What steps can you take to renew your thinking in this area?

DIV-OTION

In many instances, we will not find immediate answers or quick fixes for our situations. We must dig in our heels and make the best of a difficult situation. The question we must answer is, Are we willing to do the necessary work to choose joy over depression and hope over despair? Will you remain stuck or will you be victorious?

Re-read Jeremiah 29:4-13. As you read this portion of Scripture, reflect on a situation in your own life that makes you feel stuck or in bondage. Perhaps it's not that obvious, but you are not really content with where you are. Based on God's instructions to His people at this difficult time, note what you need to address in your own life, and write out your own personal confession.

- I will work on building...

- I will learn to accept where I am presently, knowing it is only for a season. I will settle these things in my heart...

- As I lay the foundation for my future, knowing that I will reap and eat what I sow, I will choose to plant...

- I will work on the following relationships...

- I will seek to be fruitful and not decrease in the following areas...

- I will cease from negative confessions about my situation and will no longer cast blame. I will seek to bless and be a blessing to...

- I will not allow myself to be deceived by counsel I want to hear. I will seek the truth from...

- I will be realistic about my circumstance. Because acknowledging the truth is the first step to freedom, I will be honest with myself and God first. The truth of the matter is...

- I will trust in God's plans for me and stop trying to fix...

- I will call upon, pray to, and seek the Lord with my whole heart. I will wait upon Him with a...

Diva Resources

Get Over It and On With It by Michelle McKinney Hammond

What Becomes of the Brokenhearted by Michelle McKinney Hammond

When Your Heart Aches by Lois Raby

Confessions of a Grieving Christian by Zig Ziglar

Shattered Dreams by Larry Crabb

WEEK EIGHT:
The Importance of Avoiding Foolishness

PREPARATION

Read *The Diva Principle,* pp. 69–79; 1 Samuel 25; Judges 13–16.

> *The mouths of fools are their ruin; their lips get them into trouble* (Proverbs 18:7).

My girlfriend Pamela Shine always says, "If people knew better, they would do better." In most cases, I believe this is true for those who really want change to occur in their lives. Then there is the camp of those who actually believe their foolishness is right and continue on their path of self-destruction—all in the name of doing it "my way." Sometimes those who desire change get stuck with someone who doesn't. Don't fall prey to their folly. Refuse to go to "fool's paradise" with them; rise above the fray, and stay on course. Let's take a closer look at how to recognize the signs and ensure we don't get caught up in the madness. Most importantly, how to keep our heads when everyone else is losing theirs.

OBSERVATION

1. What two traits did Nabal and Samson both possess?

2. How did Nabal's hot temper endanger his entire household?

3. What did the servant say about Nabal?

4. How was Abigail's reputation different from her husband's?

5. What was Abigail's immediate response when she heard about the trouble between Nabal and David?

6. What did Abigail remain focused on?

7. How did her level-headed approach diffuse a bad situation?

8. How did David regard Abigail as a woman?

9. What was Abigail's posture toward her husband upon arriving home and the following morning?

10. What was Nabal's reaction to Abigail's intervention? How did it affect his health?

11. How did God choose to reward Abigail for remaining in the right position in difficult circumstances?

12. What common theme about fools do these scriptures share?

    a. Proverbs 10:23

    b. Proverbs 29:11

    c. Proverbs 12:15

    d. Proverbs 12:16

    e. Proverbs 15:5

    f. Proverbs 18:2

    g. Proverbs 26:11

    h. Ecclesiastes 10:3

13. Why is self-control important?

14. What was the calling on Samson's life according to the angel (Judges 13:3-5)? Is that the first thing you think of when you hear Samson's name mentioned? Why not?

15. What guided Samson's choice of a mate?

16. Why did Samson's parents object to his choice?

17. What warning sign was Samson given on his way to his marriage?

18. What secrets did Samson keep from his parents?

19. What message do you think God was trying to send to Samson in his encounter with the lion?

20. How did Samson's bride betray him? (Judges 14:10-17)

21. What was Samson's response? What deception crept into his thinking? (Judges 15:3)

22. How did his anger affect other people? His loved ones?

23. How many relationships did Samson have with Philistine women? How did they end? Was there a common thread?

24. What similarities did Samson's wife and Delilah share? Did Samson notice these similarities?

25. What were the consequences of Samson failing to notice the warning signs in his relationship with Delilah?

26. What did Samson take for granted about God? (Judges 16:20)

27. What was the turning point for Samson?

28. What did Samson's foolishness cost him?

REFLECTION

Sometimes foolishness is not easy to spot. It can be as simple as not realizing there is safety in a multitude of counselors or not thinking before one reacts. Think about your response in situations that push your buttons. In the midst of high drama, Abigail was a woman who chose her battles wisely and eventually won the war. What cues can you take from her for your own life?

1. How does anger affect your ability to think rationally?

2. Why is refusing to listen to reason or to other people dangerous?

3. Why is it important to think before you speak, act, or react?

4. What happens when you overreact or react without thinking?

5. How does one choose which battles to fight? What should be the determining factor?

6. How can self-involvement mar your judgment?

7. How do God's agenda and your desires fit together?

8. What happens when your desires scream louder than God's still, small voice?

9. What causes you to stop being transparent with others? What happens when you stop being accountable to others?

10. Do you have a pattern of unhealthy choices or relationships in your own life?

11. What blind spots do you have? What causes them?

12. What steps can you take to avoid falling into the same trap over and over again?

DIV-OTION

Sometimes it doesn't take another fool to cause us to behave foolishly. At times, even our own heart deceives us. If we refuse the counsel of others or fail to be accountable to those who walk with us, we can find ourselves blinded by our flesh and caught up in a maze of deception that eventually leads to drama, crisis, bondage, or even death in some form—physical, spiritual, or emotional.

Here are some steps we can take to avoid foolishness.

- Examine your desires or responses to issues in the light of God's Word. Is your desire or response in keeping with God's instructions?

- Consider the counsel of those who are wise, whether or not you like what they have to say. Weigh what they counsel in the light of God's Word.

- Watch for red flags and warnings. Do not discount them. Slow your pace until you can confirm or resolve your apprehensions.

- Do not get caught up in playing games or seeking moments of immediate but temporary gratification.

- Don't use someone else's offense as an excuse for your own bad behavior. Don't try to justify behaving in an ungodly fashion. Quickly reel in thoughts of retaliation.

- Learn your lessons and don't repeat them.

- Don't allow your flesh to rule your choices. Ask yourself how God would feel about what you are doing.

- Listen to the warnings of the Holy Spirit. Be aware of cyclical behavior.

- Be quick to repent and get back on track with God.

Just Enough Light for the Step I'm On by Stormie Omartian

Foolproofing Your Life by Jan Silvious

Big Girls Don't Whine by Jan Silvious

Liberated Through Submission by P.B. Wilson

When Pleasing Others Is Hurting You by Dr. David Hawkins

WEEK NINE:

Leaving a Legacy of Servanthood

PREPARATION

Read *The Diva Principle,* pp. 81–93; Luke 1:26-38; Genesis 12:1-4; and John 13:1-16.

When you bow down before the Lord and admit your dependence on him, he will lift you up and give you honor (James 4:10).

Though the honor of being a servant has diminished in modern times, it is important to keep in mind that in God's kingdom, the way up is down. The last shall be first, the least will be greatest...you know all the famous lines. The principle of servanthood is worth its weight in gold. How does one become a leader? By first learning how to follow. Throughout Scripture, we see men and women of humble beginnings rising to great heights. Those who served became kings and queens, while those who started at the top usually finished at the bottom of the heap. Why? Because of their attitude. An attitude of entitlement will get you nowhere in a hurry.

Let's consider some of the requirements for catching God's eye, currying His favor, and receiving promotion from Him. We will take a look at what to do and what *not* to do. But first, let's study Mary and see what things stand out that made her a true servant of God whose legacy of submission remains today. I'm sure you'll agree that the traits we will study are not the usual ones you would think about when someone says the word "servant." They are described by simple words like sensitivity, purity, availability, trust, courage, and sacrifice.

OBSERVATION

1. According to Luke 1:28, what other quality did Mary possess besides her youth?

2. When the angel appeared to Mary, did she seem to find this unusual? What caused her more concern—his appearing or what he said?

3. What was Mary's response to the angel's news?

4. What can we learn from Mary's response to Gabriel?

5. What was Abraham's response when God told him to leave his home? (Genesis 12:4)

6. What character traits did Abraham's obedience display?

7. What does John 13 tell us that Jesus knew about Himself?

8. What five things did Jesus do after supper?

9. What did Peter say?

10. How did Jesus respond to Peter?

11. What example was Jesus giving the disciples?

REFLECTION

The Bible is full of amazing examples of servanthood. Do you reflect the image of a servant? Putting the needs of someone else before your own may be the best way to leave a lasting legacy of servanthood.

1. What could have made Mary so at ease in the presence of an angel?

2. What attributes made her a vessel that God could trust?

3. What was Mary risking by answering God's call?

4. Did the risks cause Mary to hold back even for a moment?

5. What sacrifice would Mary eventually have to make?

6. What is Mary's attitude?

7. Why would Peter think it was wrong for Jesus to wash his feet?

8. Consider Jesus' actions when He washed the disciples' feet. What did each step signify?

9. What sacrifice was involved in taking on the filth of others?

10. Make a list of seven people who sacrificially gave their lives for others. Describe the legacy each one left behind. (They can be biblical or historical—for example, Mother Teresa gave her life for the comfort of the

starving of India. She left behind the example of servanthood and unconditional Christian love.)

11. What legacy would you like to leave behind?

12. Write out what you would like people to say about you after you go to be with the Lord.

13. What would you need to do now in order to ensure that memory of you?

14. Consider your present spiritual life. How can you be more sensitive to the voice of the Lord?

15. In what ways can you nurture a servant's heart in your own life?

16. Why must leaders be servants first?

17. Who has God assigned you to serve? What are you doing to effect positive change in their lives? What could you do more of? What should you do less of?

DIV-OTION

When the world screams loudly, we must quiet our hearts to hear the still, small voice of God giving us direction. We cannot birth the promises of God into our lives. We must plug into the Power Source, the Giver of life, the One who gives promotion. He waits, holding abundant blessings in His hands. We need only receive them.

- Pick a time to get with God and practice silence.

- Journal the impressions He puts on your heart and the scriptures that come to mind during your quiet time.

- Begin to practice the art of listening for the voice of God in the little things.

- Start writing down what you notice.

- Prayerfully choose someone to make yourself available to. Ask God what you can do to enhance that person's life.

Diva Resources

Finding Your Purpose as a Mom by Donna Otto

A Woman After God's Own Heart by Elizabeth George

Jesus in Blue Jeans by Laurie Beth Jones

Life Design 101

*You should be known for the
beauty that comes from within, the
unfading beauty of a gentle and
quiet spirit, which is so precious to
God. That is the way the holy
women of old made themselves
beautiful (1 Peter 3:4-5).*

%⊙ ℊ

It's amazing how looking good can affect how you feel and vice versa. As I noted in my book *101 Ways to Get and Keep His Attention,* most men surveyed said they were not adamant about a woman being a size two. What they found attractive was a woman who liked the skin she was in. A woman who is healthy, fit, and feeling good about herself is very appealing. But how many of us really feel that way? Above all of the external issues are the internal ones. Attitude is key. I've met plenty of men and women who were pretty...but ugly, if you know what I mean. The secret is to cultivate both inner and outer beauty. We live in a society that has nurtured the concept that if you are beautiful you don't have to be anything else. However, outward beauty fades, but internal beauty stands the test of time. So how about nurturing both for a double whammy threat? After all, it is possible to be inwardly, outwardly, and spiritually beautiful! It all depends on you—and your willingness to do the work.

Developing True Beauty

PREPARATION

Read *The Diva Principle,* pp. 97–120; Book of Esther; Daniel 1–3; Genesis 1:29-30; and Leviticus 3:17; 7:24; 11; 17:4; 25:1-7,18-23; 26:14,33-35.

In today's competitive atmosphere, many women struggle with how to win the beauty contest, but the book of Esther makes it clear that beauty definitely has to be more than skin deep. After all the women went through the rigors of beautification, one stood out from the crowd—a submitted young woman who seemed to appear from nowhere. Her countenance and disposition were the additional stand-out features I'm sure most of the other women in the court had overlooked. The bottom line? Pretty is as pretty does. True beauty comes from trusting God to secure the desires of your heart, as well as your position in life. This frees you to walk in quiet beauty while celebrating others around you. A woman who masters this beauty secret always win the prize!

OBSERVATION

1. What four things does Esther 2 tell us the eunuch Haggai ordered for Esther?

2. What beauty treatment was prescribed for all of the women?

3. What happened the evening each woman was to appear before the king?

4. What did Esther do differently when it was her turn to see the king?

5. What were the results?

6. When Esther found out about the trouble her people were in, what did she decide to do before seeing the king?

7. After three days, what did Esther do? What was the king's response to her?

8. How did Esther win the king's attention? How did she use her beauty to her advantage?

9. How did serving the king before raising her own concerns help her get the help she needed?

10. According to Daniel 1, what were the seven requirements for selecting the young men who were chosen to go to the king's palace?

11. What were they assigned to learn?

12. What were they assigned to eat?

13. How long was their training period? What were they trained to do?

14. What did Daniel choose to eat instead? For how long?

15. What were the results?

16. In Genesis 1:29-30, what did God tell man to eat? What were the animals to eat? Compare this to Genesis 9:1-4.

17. Make a list of what man was allowed to eat according to the verses in Leviticus.

18. Make a list of what man was *not* allowed to eat according to the verses in Leviticus.

19. What was God's mandate concerning rest?

20. What would be the consequences of not resting?

REFLECTION

Rest seems to be the elusive goal for most. However, it is imperative we take the time to refresh and renew ourselves—spirit, body, and mind. Rest is the secret beautifier. It affects our appearance, our mood, and even our faith level. Small wonder God commands us to take a Sabbath.

1. Why would God insist on us getting rest?

2. What happens when you don't get the rest you need?

3. How does ignoring God's command to rest affect others around you? Your work? Your concentration? Your performance level?

4. What happens when you eat poorly? How do you feel? How does your body look? How does this affect your mood or self-esteem?

5. How can ill health and low self-esteem affect your relationships?

6. How does good health affect you mentally? Spiritually? Physically?

7. Why is it important for you to take control of your body and personal health?

8. In what ways is physical beauty an asset when dealing with people in the world?

9. Why is inner beauty crucial?

10. What are your usual steps for problem solving?

11. What have been the results?

12. How does trusting God and being at rest in His promises affect your behavior, especially in tough situations? If you struggle with trusting Him, how are you likely to act?

13. What results from your attitude of confidence or fear?

14. How can you practice resting in Him and allowing Him to intervene in your life more?

DIV-OTION

How you feel relies on the habits you cultivate and the thoughts you entertain. Sometimes we feel guilty when we take time to care for ourselves, but we have to stop and recharge our battery if we are to finish the race that is set before us. Nurturing a healthy body, spirit, and mind will equip us for the journey of life and empower us to maintain healthy relationships and function well in the marketplace. Cast down the lies of the enemy that accuse you of vanity. Adopt the attitude that you are the curator for a valuable work of art God has left in your care—your body, His temple.

- Take stock of your diet.

- Note how you feel physically. Review the list of do's and don'ts for eating biblically, and note the way your system reacts to the food you eat.

- If unsure, eliminate everything down to fruits and vegetables for a week. Then, begin to add back in things you normally eat. This can alert you to problem foods.

- Take time to rest. Kill all guilt concerning not doing anything and begin to embrace your times of rest as preparation for productivity.

- Write out goals for the way you want your body to feel and look.

- Write out a realistic plan for achieving your goals.

- Find someone to walk in agreement and accountability with you. Take it one day at a time.

- While you are taking care of the outside, don't forget the inside.

- Set aside a time for resting with God and reading His Word. Nourish your spirit just as regularly as you nourish your body.

- Write a prayer of release to God for anything you are anxious about. Find a scripture that promises you an answer for your situation and memorize it. Whisper it to your spirit until you are peaceful about your situation.

> Take a day to get a free makeover at a store every four months. Makeup trends and colors change seasonally, so get a fresh look quarterly. Even a new lipstick can give you an inner lift as well as a new smile.

Diva Resources

Even God Rested by Kim Thomas

Intended for Pleasure by Ed Wheat

Romancing Your Husband by Debra White Smith

Fit for Life by Harvey Diamond

The Answer Is in Your Blood Type by Joseph Christiano and Steven Weissberg

Thrive: A Woman's Guide to a Healthy Lifestyle by Carrie Carter, M.D.

WEEK ELEVEN:
Balancing
Work and Worship

PREPARATION

Read *The Diva Principle,* pp. 121–131; Acts 16:11-40; and Daniel 5–6.

To be or not to be? That is the question, or should I say that *was* the question! I believe the modernized version of Shakespeare's famous statement is to *do* or not to *do*. We are all so busy *doing* that we have lost the art of *being* who we were created to be—true worshippers of God, worshipping in spirit and living out the truth of our worship experience. When life is in the right order, everything else flows in a much easier fashion. Small wonder Jesus stole away to pray at the beginning and end of each day— in the morning to get grounded for the day and in the evening to refuel His engines. Many of us are burned-out from working in overdrive, and prayer falls by the wayside. The more we operate in the flesh, solely according to our own intellect, the harder we end up working. The cycle makes us feel as if we are on a treadmill with no off button. How do we balance productivity in heaven and on earth? Well, that's what we are about to explore.

OBSERVATION

1. Where did Paul meet Lydia?

2. What were they doing at the riverbank?

3. What happened after Paul spoke to the women?

4. What prompted Lydia to open her home to Paul?

5. What happened as they were on their way to prayer after this incident?

6. How did Paul and Silas respond to being put in jail?

7. What took place as they began to pray and sing hymns?

8. What was the jailer's response?

9. Where did Paul and Silas go after leaving the jail?

10. What was Daniel's reputation in the king's court?

11. What did the king say Daniel possessed?

12. What was Daniel's response to the king?

13. What reward did the king give Daniel?

14. What promotion filled Daniel's coworkers with envy?

15. How did Daniel's coworkers conspire to get rid of him?

16. What was the king's response to the accusations of Daniel's coworkers?

17. How did the king feel about having to punish Daniel?

18. After sentencing Daniel to the lions' den, what did the king do?

19. What happened the morning after Daniel spent the night in the lions' den?

20. How did God prove himself faithful to Daniel?

REFLECTION

Consider your own home and work environments and the way you conduct yourself in these places. What message are you sending in your habits and conversation? Is your light shining and illuminating others? Perhaps our behavior sends a louder message than our conversation.

1. What situation do Daniel and Paul both find themselves in?

2. How did Daniel and Paul respond to those who had placed them in bondage?

3. Did they try to defend themselves or seek their own rights?

4. Does your walk with God show others where you stand?

5. In what ways, if any, have you felt persecuted or ridiculed for your faith?

6. How do you respond when others question or argue about your faith?

7. What has been the result of your discussion?

8. What has worked in your interactions in times like these? What has not worked?

9. In what ways, if any, have you allowed the unbelief of coworkers, friends, or family members to alter moral values or your spiritual habits?

10. What happens when you stand firm in your convictions?

11. How can prayer affect your efforts and influence your coworkers, family, and friends?

12. How does prayer affect your productivity in the workplace?

13. What is the difference of how much you accomplish in your day when you pray? When you don't?

14. What keeps you from praying before you begin each day?

15. What can you do to become more diligent in this area?

DIV-OTION

- Reassert why you are where you are in the world as well as spiritually.

- Has your faith been effective at home and at work?

- Determine what keeps you from growing spiritually.

- Locate which things pull at you the most. Decide if they are profitable to your life and witness.

- Honestly pinpoint your top priority.

- Make a list of the things that rob you of living in balance.

- Write down the steps you are going to take to re-prioritize and keep balance in your life.

- Get an accountability partner to help you keep on track.

- Get an official prayer partner and set a time when you will pray for ten minutes on a daily basis. (You will go longer, trust me!)

- Keep a journal of your prayers and God's answers.

Diva Resources

Experiencing God by Henry Blackaby and Claude King

Face to Face by Kenneth Boa

Streams in the Desert by Mrs. Charles E. Cowman

My Utmost for His Highest by Oswald Chambers

Come Away My Beloved by Francis Roberts

Living the Message by Eugene Peterson

Where Are You, God? by Michelle McKinney Hammond

Having Grace in Spite of Life

PREPARATION

Read *The Diva Principle,* pp. 133–146; 2 Kings 4:8-37; 8:1-6; and Genesis 37:1–41:52.

> *So don't get tired of doing what is good. Don't get discouraged and give up, for we will reap a harvest of blessing at the appropriate time* (Galatians 6:9).

Into every life some rain must fall. Disappointment is inevitable, but our response to it is totally our choice. Our reaction will invite either victory or defeat to visit us. I dare to say that women are survivors by nature. But does one want to settle for being merely a survivor? Wouldn't you rather advance to the next level of flourishing, regardless of where life plants you? Being an overcomer? That's what I'm talking about! Reaching higher every time you feel your spirit sinking. Digging deeper every time you feel your circumstances are overwhelming you. Being gracious under fire. Reaching out to others when everything within you suggests you fold inward and sink in the mire of yourself and your issues. How do you hold your head up when you would rather weep instead? How do you anticipate better tomorrows in spite of your undesirable today? How do you delight in the Lord when you are not delighted with the way life is treating you? It all starts with a positive frame of mind.

OBSERVATION

1. What was the Shunammite woman's status in life when she met Elisha?

2. Why did Elisha want to give her a gift?

3. What was her response when he asked her what he could give her?

4. How did he conclude what to give to her?

5. What was her response? What happened next?

6. What happened to the child?

7. What did she do?

8. Who did she tell about the death of her child?

9. What was Elisha's response?

10. What request did she make of Elisha? Did he honor it?

11. When the child was brought back to life, what was the first thing his mother did?

12. In 2 Kings 8:1-6, how was her previous loss turned into an even greater blessing?

13. Read Genesis 37:9-11. Describe Joseph's dream.

14. What were Joseph's father's and brothers' responses to his dream?

15. What did Joseph's brothers' envy and jealousy cause them to do?

16. According to Genesis 39, who was with Joseph?

17. What did God do for Joseph in Potiphar's house?

18. How did Potiphar's wife behave toward Joseph? What was his response to her?

19. How did she handle his rejection?

20. What was Joseph's punishment?

21. What did the Lord do for Joseph in the jail?

22. What prompted Joseph's release from jail?

23. What was Joseph's response to Pharaoh's request that Joseph interpret Pharaoh's dreams?

24. What was Pharaoh's response?

REFLECTION

Many people have questioned the truth of God's Word. If we wait on the Lord, will He really give us the desires of our heart? It seems the road toward your dreams and desires can be long and wearisome. If we persevere and faint not, the reward comes in unexpected moments like the dawning of a new day—softly, silently, beautifully, and more splendid than we anticipated. While you wait, the choices you make are extremely important to the process of personal refining that you'll need in order to be ready for the blessing when it comes.

1. How do you think the Shunammite woman dealt with her desire for having a child? Where did she turn her attentions? Why?

2. Do you think her relationship with Elisha changed after she had the child?

3. Do you think she doubted God after the death of her child?

4. Based on her reaction to her son's death, what might she have been thinking? Why didn't she tell anyone else about the child's death?

5. After the child was brought back to life, what change in perspective do you think the Shunammite woman had? How was her relationship with Elisha changed?

6. What do you think helped Joseph to maintain a good attitude and a spirit of excellence during his long trial?

7. Why do you think God allowed Joseph to go through what he did before making his dream come true?

8. How did God complete the work in Joseph that transformed him into a wise and thoughtful man?

9. What is your heart attitude toward God?

10. Do you believe God will give you the desire of your heart?

11. Have you shared your desire with others?

12. What was their reaction or advice? Was it helpful?

13. What do you feel that God is saying to you about your desire?

14. What is your reaction to having to wait?

15. Are you actively preparing yourself to receive and handle the blessing you want?

16. When you have received other blessings you wanted, how did your relationship with God change?

17. What do you think God is trying to perfect in you as you wait for the desire of your heart?

18. What changes do you need to made in your attitude?

19. What areas of your hope need to be rebuilt?

20. How has God proven His faithfulness to you in the past on other issues that seemed impossible at the time?

DIV-OTION

Nurturing a listening and grateful heart toward God helps you wait for the promise of fulfillment in your life. The next step to keeping your peace while you wait is losing yourself in service to others. Getting over ourselves propels us closer to our dream. Occupying life to the fullest until the dream comes is mastering the art of overcoming— no matter what doubt the enemy of your soul would try to send your way.

- Make a list of things you have trouble waiting for the answers to.

- Find someone to bless and give of yourself to while you wait.

- Continue the dialogue with God until you are peaceful about waiting.

- Select and memorize scriptures that will gird up your faith.

- Get a faith partner to stand in agreement with you.

- Thank God in advance for the answer you're waiting for. Be ready!

Diva Resources

The Dream Giver by Bruce Wilkinson

Grace Amazing by Steve McVey

The Purpose-Driven Life by Rick Warren

The Power of a Praying Woman by Stormie Omartian

Act Design 101

*There is a time for everything, a season for
every activity under heaven. A time to be
born and a time to die. A time to plant and
a time to harvest. A time to kill and a time
to heal. A time to tear down and a time to
rebuild. A time to cry and a time to laugh.
A time to grieve and a time to dance. A time
to scatter stones and a time to gather stones.
A time to embrace and a time to turn away.
A time to search and a time to lose. A time to
keep and a time to throw away. A time to tear
and a time to mend. A time to be quiet and a
time to speak up. A time to love and a time to
hate. A time for war and a time for peace*
(Ecclesiastes 3:1-8).

              � ◎ ⁀℗

*L*ife is the big picture. Each of our choices and
experiences is a stroke of the brush on the huge
canvas of our years. How we wield the brush can
determine the beauty or the unattractiveness of what we, and
others, finally witness. We can only keep up appearances

so long before the real deal is exposed for all to see. And you never know who is watching. The secret to mastering life is to deal with one thing at a time, one season at a time. Doing what you can and leaving the rest to God. It is this divine partnership that helps us to finally get our act together.

Applying the Finishing Touch

PREPARATION

Read *The Diva Principle,* pp. 149–191; and Proverbs 31.

The old folks used to say, "If your act ain't tight, it ain't right." There is a lot of truth in that. Many rationalize that if one area of their life is together, they are excused from having to be diligent in others. However, just as the body works together in one unit, relying on support from all the other parts, our lives also become more cohesive when we exercise balance and nourish every part. As women, many in our inner circle rely on us as a source to draw from. We must be equipped for the task at hand with either personal knowledge and experience or the resources for getting the job done.

Beauty on its own is not enough to sustain life and all of its complexities. Neither is charm. A divine diva must have her relationship with God intact, along with wisdom, knowledge gleaned from practice and experience, and a strong support system. No woman can go it alone. Superwoman has hung up her cape. Being realistic is the first step to dealing with life effectively. Taking stock of abilities, strength, and weaknesses is vital to making honest assessments of your needs in order to move forward.

OBSERVATION

1. What does Proverbs 31 tell us is the price of a virtuous and capable wife?

2. What four things does her husband experience because of her presence in his life?

3. What does she do to take care of her household?

4. What entrepreneurial things is she involved in?

5. How does she handle her finances?

6. How does she take care of herself?

7. What are her character traits?

8. What does she do for others outside of her home?

9. How does she instruct others?

10. What is her reputation?

11. What is her husband's reputation?

12. List her priorities in order.
   a.

   b.

   c.

   d.

   e.

REFLECTION

Gazing over the laundry list and noting the Proverbs 31 woman planned her work carefully, it is safe to say that this was a disciplined woman. Many of us fly by the seat of our pants through life and wonder why we can't land on a plan. The Bible tells us to write the vision and make it plain so that a herald can run with it (Habakkuk 2:2). Having a plan is the first step to completing a vision...it's how one gets her act together.

1. If you are married, how would your husband evaluate you?

2. If you are single, how would your friends and coworkers evaluate you?

3. What things do you do to take care of yourself? Your household? Others outside of your home?

4. Do you have a solid plan for your life? For your household?

5. What are your passions? How can you mold them into something that profits you and blesses others?

6. How organized are you? What keeps you from being more organized?

7. What guidelines can you put in place in order to be more efficient in handling all your responsibilities?

8. What keeps you from putting these into place?

9. What type of help can you draw from? What chores can you delegate?

10. What long-standing projects do you need to complete before adding anything new to your list?

11. What is the state of your finances?

12. What are your areas of weakness when handling money?

13. What financial goals do you have?

14. How would you rate your homemaking skills on a scale of 1 to 10?

15. What would you like to improve in your home?

16. What would you need to do to make that happen?

17. What small touches could make a big difference right now?

18. What is your attitude toward cooking? Why? What would make it a more enjoyable experience for you?

19. What realistic goal could you set regarding cooking meals?

20. What special thing will you do to make your husband feel more nurtured this week? Your children? Yourself? Someone in need?

DIV-OTION

In order to set your life in order, your priorities must be in order. Make the time to take stock of the life you live and be honest with yourself about what you would like to do better. Make a plan that is both realistic and conducive to your personality. Don't despair over the past—you can't do anything about that. Make today the date for your new beginning. Remember, organization and discipline are key to mastering a smooth life!

   ☙ Prioritize the things you have to do. List them in order of importance.

- Note how much time is involved with each entry. Now re-prioritize according to which ones will be easier to finish quickly.

- Indicate which jobs can be delegated to others. Make a schedule for yourself of when you will start and complete each task.

- Build rest time into your list of responsibilities.

- Refrain from planning new projects until the old ones are completed.

- Seek out a financial advisor to get you on the right track with your money.

- Pinpoint the little purchases you make that add up in the long run. Eliminate those that are not really necessary.

- Enlist the help of a friend who is good at decorating to add new pizzazz to a room in your home.

- Practice a new recipe this week.

Diva Resources

Language of Love by Gary Smalley

Debt-Free Living by Larry Burkett

Tiptionary by Mary Hunt

The Courage to Be Rich by Suze Orman

The Act of Marriage by Tim and Beverly LaHaye

Intimate Issues by Lorraine Pintus and Linda Dillow

Sheet Music by Dr. Kevin Leman

Divorce-Proofing Your Marriage by Linda Mintle, Ph.D.

From One Diva to Another

As we know Jesus better, his divine power gives us everything we need for living a godly life. He has called us to receive His own glory and goodness! And by that same mighty power, he has given us all of his rich and wonderful promises. He has promised that you will escape the decadence all around you caused by evil desires and that you will share in his divine nature. So make every effort to apply the benefits of these promises to your life (2 Peter 1:3-5).

❧ ◉ ☙

*L*adies, if you've been diligent in processing the work in this guide, you have crossed over into diva-hood. Remember, being a diva is no walk in the park—it is work. It requires discipline, grace, and a healthy, heaping serving of elbow grease. Yes, we are all works in progress, so don't be disappointed if it takes a little time to shine the way you want to. Please stay encouraged and encourage others. You'll be surprised how helping others speeds up the process of growing yourself. Take advantage of all the resources that have been listed. They will give you extra wisdom and empower you to take the bold steps you will need to take in order to live the life you want.

Last, but not least, as you take steps to become a truly divine diva, prayerfully plan your work and work your plan. Allow the Holy Spirit to lead you in the way that you should go, and you won't be able to miss the victory! Be encouraged and know that you look *mah-velous, dah-ling!*

In His Divine Love,
Michelle

% ⊙ ℘

Other Books by
Michelle McKinney Hammond

What to Do Until Love Finds You
Secrets of an Irresistible Woman
Where Are You, God?
The Power of Being a Woman
Get a Love Life
If Men Are Like Buses, Then How Do I Catch One?
Prayer Guide for the Brokenhearted
What Becomes of the Brokenhearted?
How to Be Blessed and Highly Favored
Get Over It and On With It
Wounded Hearts, Renewed Hope
Why Do I Say "Yes" When I Need To Say "No"?
Sassy, Single, & Satisfied
The Unspoken Rules of Love
In Search of the Proverbs 31 Man
101 Ways to Get and Keep His Attention
The D.I.V.A. Principle

To correspond with Michelle McKinney Hammond,
you may write to her:
c/o Heartwing Ministries
P.O. Box 11052
Chicago, IL 60611
E-mail her at heartwingmin@yahoo.com
Or log on to her website at:
www.michellemckinney.com
or www.heartwing.org

For information on booking her for a
speaking engagement:
Contact Speak Up Speaker Services at
1-888-870-7719